The Ultimate Cognitive Behavioral Therapy Guide to a Better, Healthier, Happier YOU

Manage Depression, Insomnia, Anxiety, OCD, Intrusive Thoughts, Procrastination, Addiction, & Jealousy

By Robert L. Rogers

ISBN:

Table of Contents

Introduction

When it comes to mental health care, there are many varieties of therapy and practices a trained professional can use to help their patients reach their goals. One of the most common varieties of therapy used in today's day and age is cognitive behavioral therapy, also known as CBT. This model of therapy uses an evidence-based model with a long-proven history to help individuals meet countless goals, whether they be to lessen general anxiety throughout a person's day-to-day life or address specific concerns such as phobias.

Please keep in mind that no form of therapy is one-size-fits-all. When working to improve your mental health, it is important to keep in mind your specific needs and worries. This means that if a standard recommendation for therapy isn't quite what you need, you can customize it to better fit your struggles and needs. If, at first, you don't succeed, don't become discouraged! Instead, work toward resolving any struggles to find what best fits you as an individual. The great news for you is that by learning about CBT in this book, you will find that this process becomes easier. You will learn how to pinpoint your struggles and how to overcome them for mental health. I will walk you through the cognitive–behavioral therapy process so that you can achieve the results you desire.

While reading this book, you might benefit from bookmarking specific passages and workbook pages to refer back to from time to time. This is helpful, as progress is not linear. You may seem to be making progress for a time, only to backtrack from time to time. This is a perfectly common struggle and nothing to be discouraged about! When this happens, simply refer back to your bookmarked pages in this book and analyze what needs are not being met and how you can overcome your struggles. If you do this, you will find that you continue to make progress. Eventually, you will be able to admire your results, as you will be able to clearly see how you have grown closer to or met your goals altogether.

Lastly, as you read through this book, please remember to take your time. Your goals and progress cannot be rushed. Otherwise, you will become overwhelmed, and your progress will halt. Take growth one step at a time, staying in tune with your mental health needs and personalizing the speed at which you work through this book to optimize your growth. Every person will have a different speed than they have to approach this book. Some may be able to speed through it and remember all the important information, whereas others may need to slowly take their time to absorb all the information, and that is okay! Take it at your own pace that allows you to fully understand and absorb the lessons that will allow you to successfully grow and reach your mental health goals.

Remember, no matter how severe your symptoms may seem or feel, you can fix things. If not through this book, then through seeking help from a licensed therapist or taking medication. No matter how bad your discomfort feels, or how hopeless it may seem at times, you can make things better. No matter how hard things may get, remember to keep your goals in mind, and never stop striving for them. Happiness and mental wellness are within your reach, even if your discomfort has fooled you into thinking otherwise.

Chapter 1:
What Is CBT?

Cognitive Behavioral Therapy

We have to face quite a few specific kinds of problems and events of life. Any of those might be nice; others might not be so fun. However, the way we live life, whether we love it or hate it, is a characteristic of the kind of perspective we have, as well as the emotional strength we can muster. Some individuals are always optimistic and positive, allowing them with power and equanimity to deal with all circumstances. There are others on the other end of the scale that are very timid and also negatively predisposed, making them quite scared, and even quite intimidated by everything.

While in some other cases, some people are cynical by nature, people also go through traumatic experiences that change their lives forever. For example, children who experience a murder or possible terrorist attack could suffer lifelong mental damage and suffer from panic and anxiety attacks. To the point where they are eternally miserable or perhaps cranky, moody, and angry all the time, surely others feel harassed and bothered as well. These are all examples of behaviorally dysfunctional actions and lifestyles that need to be addressed through cognitive behavioral therapy, also known as CBT.

CBT is a therapy through which professional clinicians and psychologists work alongside people to try to help them find the reason they are behaving in a particular way with themselves. Thoughts provide a ride into building emotions and behavior and make it essential to address ideas and also analyze them properly so that the root cause of the problem can be identified and resolved. The fundamental strategy is to replace depressive feelings with constructive and optimistic feelings before the individual has a second nature, which is positivity. Only in this way can one be healthy and happy again.

We do not take for granted that CBT is a straightforward technique. Of one, it needs a lot of meticulous and long-drawn psychoanalysis methods, as well as psychiatric therapy such that old memories and deteriorating or wounded emotions will be allowed to disappear into the past. This will help bring happiness to the forefront and help a person make rational and healthy choices too. After all, ensuring that life is lived to the fullest without regrets is crucial.

How Does CBT Work?

Cognitive-behavioral therapy has a six-phase approach to helping people heal the mental conditions that they are dealing with. The goal is to recognize the cognitive distortions they are experiencing and identify ways to overcome these cognitive distortions by ultimately creating stronger coping methods, cognition, emotions, and behaviors. The goal is to develop people who are more adaptive and capable of being involved in the real world with less problematic experiences in their emotions and cognitions.

The entire cycle of CBT starts with recognizing what the problematic behaviors and experiences are, and using those to identify the challenging cycles that people are facing in their minds, which lead to these actions and experiences. After that, the individual learns CBT-based techniques that are meant to help them navigate those thoughts, feelings, and behaviors healthily and more effectively. Through that, they can begin changing their problematic cycles, which results in them experiencing newer, less troubling processes in their lives.

Basic CBT Framework

CBT relies on a basic framework that follows six phases. These six phases are meant to draw a map for how the individual is going to get from where they are now to where they want to be. This entire forward-focus of CBT is what leads to individuals having such a great benefit from CBT as it supports them with coping and healing going forward, rather than placing excessive emphasis on what has happened in the past.

Phase One: Assessment

The first phase in CBT is to assess what the problem is and get a full scope understanding of what this problem is leading to an individual's life. The idea is to create a map of parts that shows where the problem is starting and what it is leading to every single time it takes place. Usually, in this phase, people see that their issues are leading to situations that are causing more of the same problem to keep recurring.

Getting a full and clear understanding of what the problem is and what the situation entails is essential, as this is the entire foundation upon which the individual will be able to begin changing their experiences. You need to make sure that you have everything in place and clearly understood so that you can identify the proper strategies that are going to support you in healing the ailments that have caused you to seek treatment in the first place.

Phase Two: Reconceptualization

The next part of the CBT framework is reconceptualization. Often, once people identify the cycles of their problems, they realize that in their minds, they feel as though things could not possibly go in any other way. The idea is that the way things are now is unchangeable, and people will always continue to have these experiences and feel this way, and there is nothing that can be done about it. Of course, this same set of beliefs leads to them feeling trapped in the first place because they are incapable of seeing that there are other possibilities for how things could go or what could be done to break the cycle.

During the reconceptualization phase, the entire purpose is to identify what can be changed about the individual's present belief system to make one that is much more supportive of their goals in life. This way, they can begin to see beyond their limited perspective and limiting beliefs and start to see into a new truth or a new way of thinking that supports them in breaking the cycle. In some cases, the belief shift is slight, whereas, in others, an entirely new way of perceiving and believing may be required to help the person ultimately move on from that way of behaving.

Phase Three: Skills Acquisition

Now, the individual has identified the new goals and new way of perceiving their reality. They need to move into acquiring skills that can help them reinforce these new beliefs in their life. Often, people do not believe in a different way of life, because they do not have the skills needed actually to make that way of life exist, so they think that they are incapable of getting there. When you begin to create the skills, you need to have the reality you want to have, believing that it is possible and getting there becomes a lot easier. Also, changing your mind becomes a lot easier because you no longer feel trapped within your cycles, and instead start having hope in what you may experience in the future.

Phase Four: Skills Consolidation and Application

Once you have figured out which skills will work best for you when it comes to treating your ailment, and you've practiced them, you need to start consolidating and applying them to your actual condition. This is the part of your process where you get the opportunity to bring these skills all together into one treatment, and use them to help you change your mind completely.

As you begin to consolidate your skills, you need to identify how you can reasonably apply them to your ability to overcome your ailment. This means that you need to go back to the map you drew in phase one and identify where these skills would be best used. Then prepare yourself for those circumstances by laying out how and when you will apply your new skills. Once you have created these expectations around yourself and your treatment, you can begin to implement your new skills in these areas and allow yourself to start experiencing the benefits of them.

Phase Five: Generalization and Maintenance

After you have begun routinely applying your new skills to your particular ailment, the next phase is to focus on generalization and maintenance. This is the part of CBT where you begin to learn how to take these new skills and strategies and turn them into actual routine practices that you are going to apply to your life as a habit. This is how you can begin to embrace your changes more automatically.

In addition to embracing your changes in a systematic way for your existing ailments, you also want to learn how to generalize these skills, so that you can use them for many areas of your life. Since CBT primarily focuses on stress management and stress response, these techniques can be used in many ways for people. Learning how to generalize your skills, and apply them to multiple areas of your life, can help minimize your present ailment while also supporting yourself in experiencing a healthier life overall.

Phase Six: Post-Treatment Assessment

As you continue to apply your CBT treatment to your ailment, you need to make sure that you take the time to perform a post-treatment assessment, to see if your new skills are helping you or not. Your post-treatment assessment will be done many times over until the point where you find that you have experienced significant enough relief for an extended period, which ultimately proves that you are no longer struggling.

If you go back to your old way of living and experiencing, immediately after realizing it, you will find yourself experiencing tremendous struggles in your life, as you face difficulties in your way of coping once again. You must always continue to embrace your new way of being so that you can continue to overcome the problematic ailment, while at the same time, you are preventing the development of any future complicated disorders due to poor coping methods.

Chapter 2:
CBT for Depression

The term depression has been thrown around so lightly in today's culture that it has now come to mean any feeling of sadness or lethargy. However, depression is much more serious with that, as those who struggle with it already know. Called the "common cold of mental illnesses" because of its prevalence, depression dramatically negatively affects an individual's thoughts, emotions, and behaviors.

Living with depression is like coasting through life, feeling unmotivated to do anything, and drowning in self-loathing. Most people who are depressed struggle to even get out of bed in the morning, much less do anything productive with their day.

With a variety of options to choose from on how to handle this type of psychological problem, one of the most prominent and practical methods used by multiple individuals and therapists worldwide is psychotherapy.

There are different types of psychotherapy, but the most used and found to be most helpful for patients is Cognitive Behavioral Therapy (CBT). This particular form of therapy was designed to treat depression (as you might recall from reading the "History of CBT" segment earlier. Handling a person's thought pattern, emotions, and behavioral aspects can get something more significant in life and not dwell on the negative side of everything.

CBT is a vast and complex treatment known to help treat a variety of mental illnesses, depression being one of them. Listed below are some ways each individual can use cognitive behavioral therapy when faced with different kinds of depression.

Major Depression

Major Depression is one of the most common types of depression. Approximately 16.2 million adults are suffering from it in the US alone. Also termed as "Major Depressive Disorder," "Unipolar Depression," or "Classic Depression," this kind of depression is characterized by feeling too much grief or gloom, being overly fatigued most of the time, having a hard time sleeping well at night, losing interest in activities that once excite you, not wanting to eat as much as you did before, feeling hopeless or experiencing anxiety, and perhaps contemplating about self-harm or suicide.

However, this type of depression does not typically stem from a person's surroundings or situation. A person could have everything one may dream of and still have depression.

Major Depression can last for as long as a week or possibly throughout one's entire lifetime. Causing a hindrance between their social and personal life, major depression can keep you from enjoying everything you love about life and isolate yourself from others. Negative thinking patterns may lead you to an unhealthy lifestyle.

So how do you overcome it? Cognitive Behavioral Therapy is one of the most common and effective methods therapists use to help their clients overcome their depression. Enabling the individual to alter their thought patterns, Cognitive Behavioral Therapy (CBT) faces the problem head-on and acknowledges the situation.

CBT helps you eliminate your negative thoughts and replace them with more positive ones. As it alters negative thoughts into positive ones, it also positively impacts emotions and behavior like a domino effect. It also deals with dysfunctional behaviors and changing them for the better. Some specific CBT techniques can help individuals deal with significant depression, but most experts would agree that cognitive restructuring would be the most suitable technique to apply here.

Depressed individuals tend to have negative automatic thoughts. Through cognitive restructuring, they can deal with this and replace it with more positive ones to help them function better mentally and emotionally. Here's a guide on how to use cognitive restructuring on your own:

- **Assess the situation.** Find the negative aspect that's upsetting you.

- **Keep track of your negative emotions.** Describe them in your journal and rate the intensity of each emotion.

- Would you please pay attention to all the things you automatically think of whenever you encounter a difficult situation and keep track of how much you believe in each of them?

- Examine these thoughts and see if they are realistic or not

- Generate better and positive thoughts that are realistic and seem more likely to happen when compared to your automatic thoughts.

- Evaluate the process and repeat as much as necessary.

These techniques can be beneficial in dealing with a depressive episode on your own. However, it is essential to remember that professional help can sometimes be the better option, especially when dealing with depression which can often leave the person feeling unmotivated to complete their therapy and hopeless about ever recovering from their mental illness.

Major Depression can be treated with CBT in different healthcare clinics. Individuals have to assess their state of mind, and once things become too hard for them to handle, they should talk to other people, like therapists, about their problems. This way, they can live a better life and slowly regain control.

Persistent Depression

Also identified as "dysthymia" or "chronic depression," persistent distress is the most recurrent of all types of depression, typically manifesting in episodes that last as long as two years and return throughout an individual's lifetime. It may not come as powerful as Major Depression, but it may still take its toll on the one experiencing it.

The feeling of being sad and hopeless, having second thoughts about yourself, lack of interest, and the problem of being happy during joyous occasions may be a sign of this type of depression.

It can also change your perspective on how life works. Symptoms may fade out for a while before coming back as clear and powerful as ever, making it difficult for a person to feel like they have any semblance of control over their lives. Therapy is one of the many ways to overcome this particular type of depression.

Cognitive Behavioral Therapy (CBT) can be essential in dealing with long-term depression such as persistent depression. This kind of depression may be an occasional experience for some individuals.

There are moments when they seem to be expected and happy and other times wherein, they can't seem to see the bright side to anything. When dark moments come, it is essential to use CBT in handling this situation. CBT replaces negative thoughts with positive ones and changes how one may behave in this kind of situation.

It can alter your trail of thought and behavior for you to see the better things in life. When people with persistent depression use CBT, it can be possible for them to get over this long-term illness and go on with their own life happily.

A common CBT technique that can help you get through persistent depression on your own is problem analysis. Also known as "situational analysis," it helps people see the problem objectively and find a positive solution for it. Problem analysis starts with:

- Finding the problem

- Understanding the problem and how it works

- Dividing the situation into smaller parts to understand it better

- Finding out what your goal is and what you want to work towards

- Finding positive ways to reach your goal and move on from the problem

Problem analysis can help treat persistent depression since it can help them positively overcome the problem. This CBT technique will aid them in triumphing over depression and help them on their way to recovery.

Manic Depression

Another term for Manic Depression is "bipolar disorders." This is composed of different periods called Mania and Hypomania. An individual's moods can be replaced between a state of feeling extreme euphoria and extreme depression.

There are different moods for different periods, changing without any sensible reason. Mania is a severe period that may last for around seven days which is then followed by Hypomania. This less robust experience may still cause an impact on an individual.

Different symptoms are existing to distinguish this illness, most of which are similar to major depression. However, indications of the manic phase may be increased self-confidence, destructive behavior, high energy, less sleep, and a euphoric state.

When tackling something as complex as Manic Depression, CBT can do a great job handling this illness. Directly impacting one's behavior, bipolar disorder can severely impact one's way of life and alter their actions and thought patterns.

So, CBT can be an excellent method to manage one's behavior and positively impact their thoughts to induce better moods and feelings for an individual. People with Manic Depression can overcome this illness through intensive CBT sessions and talking with other people to calm and control their mood swings.

This can help them become better and gain better control over their life again. There are a variety of CBT techniques that individuals with bipolar disorder can make use of. One of the most helpful ways in dealing with this particular type of depression is by controlling your cognitive distortions, which you can do by making sure you are not:

- **Over generalizing**—jumping to conclusions because of a single instance (i.e., you miss the shot once and immediately think that you're a terrible player and you can't play any sport well)

- **Thinking all-or-nothing**—seeing the world in terms of absolutes, meaning people or circumstances are either all good or all bad

- **Taking things too personally**—believing that everything wrong that happens is because of you (for example, "The teacher was mad at the class because I forgot my homework.")

- **Minimizing the positive**—discounting the good things that happen because you believe they are by luck or something out of your control

- **You maximize the negative**—dwelling on your failures and frustrations so much that they keep you from being happy.

This can kind of cognitive reconstruction can help individuals with manic depression overcome their depressive episodes and control their emotions.

The process allows individuals to take control of their mental strategies and change their behavior. So, individuals with this type of depression can use this process whenever they feel the need to assess their thoughts and behaviors.

Perinatal Depression

Perinatal Depression is a depressive disorder known to be experienced by pregnant women during or after their pregnancy. Also called postpartum depression, hormones produced during pregnancy can generate different mood swings and unusual behavior.

This feeling can also be increased because of the difficulties a mother must undergo after giving birth, such as lack of sleep and constant care of their newborn child. Symptoms that accompany this illness are the feeling of sadness, regular anxiety, worry regarding your baby's health, difficulty in caring for yourself or your baby, and possibly harming one's self or the baby. Postpartum depression is hazardous when left untreated.

This particular illness can endanger the mother and child's health and well-being. When dealing with Perinatal Depression, CBT can help mothers see a better outlook on life with new circumstances. This therapy can allow them to deal with their negative thoughts about their new life and replace them with positive ones that will enable them to see the bright side of things.

Cognitive Behavioral Therapy will also allow them to adjust and change their behavior that may positively impact their current situation. Through CBT, new mothers can see different methods to handle their every life and find better options on how to address various conditions favorably.

CBT can help these women deal with the way they feel and the way they handle things. CBT is a vast and complex process that involves many different procedures before actually concluding. Many other CBT techniques can help these individuals deal with their thoughts and behaviors better with this notion.

One unique CBT process that is sure to assist mothers with perinatal depression is the Thought Challenge Exercise. The process starts with this:

- Look at the situation objectively.

- Identify the feelings you possess regarding the situation and recognize them.

- Challenge your thought patterns and the way you behave by seeing the evidence.

Alter these unfavorable thoughts, emotions, and behaviors into better ones by identifying them and looking for better solutions to handle things

Situational Depression

Situational Depression may often look like Major Depression. However, it is triggered by specific scenarios or situations in life. It is known to be an adjustment disorder with a depressed mood. It may be induced by problems like the death of a loved one, a life-threatening event, abusive relationships, or financial issues.

These situations may bring about situational depression and its symptoms such as frequent crying, sadness, anxiety, social withdrawal, and over-fatigue. Situational Depression is becoming depressed over a particular event or scenario that happened or is happening in one's life. Through CBT, individuals may see a better way to cope with their situation and focus on a better and clearer thought pattern.

They may change the way they think about life in a much more positive way and control how they behave towards the situation. This type of depression can be tough to handle. When left without treatment, it may also progress in a different complex and severe mental illnesses that significantly impact one's lifestyle.

There are various CBT techniques to choose from to handle this problem. However, Journaling is known to be quite helpful and calming to do. It lets individuals assess their thoughts, improve their behavior and mood, and attain a relaxed and calm feature that will help them in the future. Effectively journaling your thoughts for depression can be done by:

- Changing your viewpoint to avoid any biases and to look at the situation objectively

- Writing down all your emotions and the way you feel about the situation

- Incorporating it into your everyday routine

- Attempt new things

- Stay focused on the positive side and ignore the negative side

- Jot down all the potential triggers for you

- List positive items daily

CBT can help these individuals achieve a better perspective in life. Simply assessing yourself and talking to others when you have a chance can significantly impact you. Talking about your illness can help you rather than shame you. It is never wrong to be fighting battles of the mind.

Chapter 3:
Behavioral Activation
and Problem Solving

The first step required to remedy a problem is to change how we react when confronted with a distressing situation. Just as the way we think and feel can trigger physical responses, our behavior can greatly affect the way we think and feel.

Go back to what you wrote about your vicious cycles; pay particular attention to what you wrote down in regards to "behaviors." We usually act automatically when under stress without thinking about the consequences of our actions. Looking at what you are used to doing to cope with your problems, make an objective assessment by answering these questions as honestly as possible and writing down your responses:

- What helped me and get through the things that are causing me distress?

- What actions did I actually take?

- What did I avoid doing?

- What automatic reactions am I prone to having?

- What were the consequences of my actions?

- Did it affect the way I feel later, and if so, how?

Formulate an Action Plan

To break a vicious cycle, you need to substitute destructive behaviors with sensible and positive actions. That is easier said than done though! However, with proper thought and planning, using what you have been journaling so far, you can start making changes in your daily life and building good habits that go a long way to keeping the negative vicious cycle from recurring.

Now, think about healthy and realistic options for dealing with distressing emotions to replace your usual behaviors. This is your personal action plan, so choose what works best for you. Write down a list of things you can do, and as you go along, ask yourself the following:

- What are the best and most helpful solutions for my situation?

- How will it help out with my problems?

- Will this/these option/s be effective and appropriate?

- Is it practical in terms of the particular event?

- Does it align with my personal beliefs, values, and principles?

- What consequences will it have in my day-to-day life?

- How will it affect my normal daily routine?

- Will others around me be involved or affected?

- By doing this, am I just avoiding my problems?

When making your action plan, you want to be mindful that your choice of activities is not a way of denying and avoiding your problems, because that will only worsen the situation. Whatever you resist will persist! The key is to find activities that will keep your thoughts occupied and make you feel better; not temporary escapism for your troubles. This means you may need to think about confronting your fears, work on kicking a bad habit of carrying out a "lifestyle overhaul," if that is what it takes to improve your well-being. Here are some suggestions of activities that can help pull us out of the self-destructive loop:

- Teach yourself to pause and take deep breaths rather than respond impulsively

- Relaxation techniques, such as deep breathing, visualization, yoga, meditation, and prayer

- Grounding techniques, like touching something tangible, holding a comforting object, and surrounding yourself with familiar sounds, scents, and sights

- Stay connected to trusted friends and family, so that you will always have someone to talk to about your problems

- Start a physical exercise routine

- **Take up a creative endeavor**—painting, learn a new music instrument, take a creative writing course or redecorate your house

- Pamper yourself; go for a massage, watch a movie, treat yourself to a nice dinner and go shopping (within your means, of course)

- Cultivate a positive inner voice; encourage yourself with affirmations like "I can do this!," "I'll be okay, this will come to pass," "I'm strong enough to go through this," "I've been through this before and I can do it again!" and "I'm better than that!"—make these self-motivating affirmations your personal mantras

Just Do It!

A plan is only good if it is actually being implemented. So, after you have your plan clearly charted out, then the obvious next step is to follow through on it. Let us be realistic, making lasting behavioral changes will not happen overnight. It will take some time for old habits to die and be replaced by new positive behaviors.

Don't set yourself up for failure. Just make an effort to start with small baby steps by doing something different from what you normally would each day, and only do as much as you can comfortably manage. As long as you are doing something—however small it may be—it's a step in the right direction. Start small and stay consistent; slowly, like a rolling snowball, your accumulated efforts will change your life for the better.

Chapter 4:
CBT for Insomnia

Insomnia

Insomnia refers to a sleep disorder that makes falling asleep difficult or staying asleep difficult. In some cases, it can cause you to wake up too early to be unable to go back to sleep. A person who doesn't get enough sleep will feel tired upon waking up. Insomnia is a serious condition that can affect your energy, mood, health, and work performance.

Although everyone is different, the recommended amount of sleep for adults is seven to eight hours each night.

Acute insomnia can occur at any time in a person's life. It can last several days to weeks. Some people experience chronic insomnia for long periods. This type of insomnia could be linked to other medical conditions.

You can beat insomnia by simply changing your daily routine. What is the best way to know if you have insomnia? There are many symptoms of insomnia. These symptoms may include:

- Finding it difficult to fall asleep during bedtime

- Sleepless nights up to halfway through the night

- Getting up very early

- Even after a good night's rest, I feel tired.

- I feel tired and sleepy during the day.

- Being anxious, irritable, and depressed

- It is difficult to stay focused, attentive, and remember what you have done.

- Having a higher rate of mistakes and accidents I am always worried about sleep.

What Is the Relationship Between Age and Insomnia?

The age of an individual's insomnia can directly relate to their health. Insomnia is more common in older people. As they age, people experience:

- **Your sleep pattern changes**—as a person ages, sleep becomes less. Slight noise or other changes in one's environment can cause a person to wake up frequently. Age causes the internal clock to advance, making one tired earlier at night and waking up even earlier. Regardless, it is healthy to have the same amount of sleep when older, just like a younger person.

  If you are less active during the day, changes in what you do may take an afternoon nap. This, in the end, will interfere with your sleep at night.

- **Change in health**—if a person experiences chronic pain from conditions like arthritis or back pains, they may have challenges sleeping. Other conditions, like anxiety or depression, also interfere with sleep. Other medical issues may cause frequent urinating at night, such as bladder problems, diabetes, among others.

- **Prescription drugs**—older people use more prescription medicines than younger people do. This increases the chance of developing chronic insomnia.

Children and teens can also be affected by insomnia. Most of these causes are due to irregular sleep patterns.

In some cases, sleep deprivation can be linked to certain risks. If:

- **The individual is a woman.** Shifts in the hormones during the menstrual cycle or menopause play a significant role. When a woman is going through menopause, they experience hot flashes and night sweats that will interrupt sleep. Pregnant mothers also experience insomnia due to hormonal changes.

- **If you are over the age of 60, then your chances of suffering from insomnia are high.** As you age, you experience changes in health, increasing the risk of insomnia.

- If you are experiencing a mental health disorder or a physical health condition, you are at a greater risk of developing insomnia.

Stress is another condition that increases insomnia. When a person is undergoing stressful situations, they may have temporary insomnia. However, prolonged periods of stress may also result in chronic insomnia in many individuals.

Lack of a regular schedule is another contributor to insomnia. A person that often travels across different time zones or works with various shifts is likely to experience insomnia.

Insomnia Complications

Healthy eating habits are essential. Regular, healthy sleep is equally important. No matter what the reason, insomnia can have a negative impact on your physical and mental health. People with insomnia experience a lower quality of life than those who have good sleeping habits.

Many complications can be associated with insomnia:

- Poor performance at work or school

- Reduced reaction time on roads that could lead to higher accidents risks

- Mental health disorders like anxiety, substance abuse, and depression

- Higher risk of long-term diseases such as heart diseases.

Practical Strategies That Will Help You Sleep Better

Good sleep habits are key to preventing insomnia and allowing you to sleep soundly. You can improve your sleep habits by following these simple steps:

- Be consistent in your bed and wake time even during the weekends.

- **Be active.** Regular physical activity will aid in promoting a good night's sleep.

- Check your medications if one of the side effects is lack of sleep. If so, speak to your doctor to switch the medicine.

- Try and avoid daytime naps, and if you feel you must, limit the duration.

- Limit or avoid the use of nicotine, alcohol, or caffeine entirely.

- Avoid taking huge meals before bedtime and taking sugary beverages.

- Don't use your bedroom as a workstation or a place for entertainment. Use it only for the intended purpose.

- You can create a relaxing bedtime routine, such as a warm bath, reading, or listening to low-volume music.

Chapter 5: CBT for Anxiety

Anxiety is the feeling of unease that an individual may feel about a certain person, object, place, or situation. Sometimes taking the form of fear or worry, anxiety is such a common feeling that it comes and goes in everyone's life.

However, some develop certain types of anxiety disorders that can lead to extreme and irrational reactions or behavioral responses. Anxiety disorders are actually psychiatric problems that can make an individual feel extreme negative emotions that can lead to unfavorable circumstances.

CBT and Anxiety

Cognitive-behavioral therapy can help treat certain real-life situations. In fact, CBT is probably one of the most recognized treatments in the industry today. CBT manages the cognitive and behavioral aspects of a person that will essentially help change their perspective and treatment of life. Through this treatment, they can understand the deeper meaning of life and exactly how to deal with specific situations that require additional effort and consideration before taking action.

CBT is adaptable to many types of psychological problems. It has a wide range of specialties in which it can be applied and used. This type of treatment has treated many mental disorders ranging from anxiety to depression to phobias. The techniques used in CBT are one of the key factors in making it useful for many diseases. It can be used to treat many types of problems and is effective for most. CBT is identified as one of the best and most positive treatments for patients with basic and complex mental disorders. Since this treatment touches the cognitive aspect of an individual, it essentially makes a bigger and more positive impact and follows through with a change with their future emotions and behavior.

Types of Anxiety

There are five main types of anxiety disorders, all of which involve certain types of anxiety and different ways of how it is triggered and addressed. Cognitive-behavioral therapy (CBT) is considered by many mental health professionals as the preferred psychosocial intervention for most of them.

In addition to its impressive effectiveness, it also helps the individual to lead a better life even with the disorder. It teaches him many valuable skills to help him deal with his conditions. Listed below are some of the anxiety disorders and how CBT can help people overcome each.

Generalized Anxiety Disorder (GAD)

One of the most prevalent anxiety disorders, Generalized Anxiety Disorder (GAD) is characterized by excessive concern for almost everything in a person's life without a particular cause or reason.

People who have GAD tend to have a big problem with everything. They become anxious about everything in their life, be it their financial status, work, family, friends, or health. They are always worried about the worry that something terrible may happen. They expect the worst-case scenario above all and always try to see things from a negative point of view.

That said, it is easy to see how GAD can make it difficult for someone to live a happy and healthy life. It can be an obstacle to your daily life and become a problem regarding your work, family, friends, and any other social activity. Some of the most common symptoms of GAD include worry or excessive tension, tiredness, inability to rest, difficulty sleeping, headaches, mood swings, difficulty concentrating, and nausea.

Yoga has been shown to help reduce a person's stress, which in turn relaxes their muscles. There are several different yoga poses and routines that you can find online designed to relieve your stress and anxiety. Some examples include eagle pose, head pose, child pose, crescent pose, and legs.

By using CBT, a person with GAD will have a much more favorable outlook on life. Rather than always worrying and thinking about the worst-case scenario, CBT reinforces an optimistic and reasonable outlook on life, which will have a positive impact on your behavior. Most of the time, they change from a tense and nervous person to a relaxed and calm person who does not assume the worst of everything.

Social Anxiety

Another common type of anxiety is social anxiety, characterized by immediate distress when you meet or interact with unknown people. Affecting more than 15 million different American adults can be considered one of the most prominent types of anxiety in the country.

Also known as "social phobia," people with social anxiety often show visible signs or symptoms that indicate their discomfort towards the situation. Some of those symptoms may include flushing, stuttering, increased heart rate, sweating, being uncomfortable or bored, and, in the worst case, experiencing a full-blown anxiety attack.

If you are one of the many people who suffer from social anxiety, you would understand how much disturbance it can have in your life. Because it prevents you from many social interactions, you may have difficulty connecting with other people and making new friends. This can also affect your personality as it can prevent you from having fun when hanging out with friends as you don't dare to stand up and speak for yourself. You are afraid to get involved in social situations and do everything possible to stay as hidden as possible and avoid interacting with other people at all costs.

Look at the current situation you are facing. Describe it to yourself. Evaluate how that particular situation made you feel and identify those feelings.

Review your thoughts about that particular scenario and explore what your mind thought immediately when you faced that situation. The first thoughts that appear in your head are your "automatic thoughts."

Panic Disorder

Panic attacks are characterized by unexpected emotions or feelings of fear when, in fact, there is no real reason to be afraid. Having recurring panic attacks for no apparent reason is what is known as panic disorder. This is mostly found in young adults age 20 and older. However, it can also be experienced by other children who also have panic symptoms.

Anxiety disorders can significantly affect a person's life. Always being at risk for spontaneous panic attacks can lead them to avoid going out and therefore isolate themselves from others. People with panic disorder generally live in fear of having another panic attack, so they do their best to control it or even hide from other people.

People with panic disorder often spend most of their time fearing the possibility of another panic attack (a fear known as "agoraphobia"). Agoraphobia is when people remain on high alert for possible panic attacks and always keep their guard up in the event of real danger. This can lead them to avoid certain places like shopping malls, festivals, cinemas, supermarkets, and the like.

Several CBT techniques can help people with panic disorder overcome their condition or calm each time a panic attack arises. Developing your calming skills is one of the most remarkable methods. If you are struggling with panic disorder, try this essential guide to ease your mind and prevent a panic attack from escalating once you feel anxiety knocking on your mind's door.

Obsessive-Compulsive Disorder

Obsessive-compulsive disorder, also known as OCD, is a psychological problem that involves uncontrollable ideas or thought patterns and behaviors that you feel compelled or have a sudden need to do. These are unwanted thoughts, obsessions, or images that enter the individual's mind and can serve as a significant discomfort that will essentially become an obstacle between the individual's daily activities and mentality. Subsequently, the individual will have no choice but to participate or perform repetitive acts and behaviors to control or deal with these thoughts.

OCD can significantly affect lifestyle. With these thoughts and compulsions, they will stop their daily activities and try to get involved or manage their feelings. This type of mental problem can start at age seven and progress later. Generally, affecting boys over women, the rate of people with OCD will increase more on the women's side in the long term. There are different types of obsessions and compulsions when it comes to OCD.

It can have a significant impact on your school, work, social, and personal life. This may allow them to have difficulty falling asleep, maintaining hygiene, forming friends, maintaining their grades, or participating in any type of social or sports performance.

There are different types of symptoms when it comes to OCD. Cognitive symptoms include continually thinking, "I am responsible for everything," "What if I get sick from this?" and "I must know everything!"

Physical symptoms, such as muscle tension, constant stomach pain, dizziness, headaches, and feeling disconnected from your body, can also be identified. For further implication that an individual has this type of psychological problem, there are also emotional symptoms that you can also check, such as anxiety, sadness, guilt, shame, and anger.

CBT tries to replace your unwanted thoughts and images with positive images and gain a much more positive outlook on life. Positive thoughts will lead to positive emotions that are likely to produce better behaviors towards situations after working on the cognitive side. This can allow them to control how they react to specific scenarios and manage their compulsion.

There are also some helpful CBT techniques that individuals may use whenever they feel those unwanted images creeping at their doorstep again or if they become unsettled by the emotions they're having. One of those techniques is by finding the root cause of your thoughts and feelings.

Post-Traumatic Stress Disorder

Post-traumatic stress disorder (PTSD) is a type of anxiety disorder that stems from traumatic, stressful, or terrifying events that can lead a person to experience traumatic episodes that force them to relive that same event.

PTSD is known to have a significant effect on people's lives. This can prevent them from trying things, going to different places, or socializing with other people regularly. A traumatic event (such as a car accident or natural calamity) can make people always think about that occasion and experience horrible setbacks, as well as nightmares. People with PTSD tend to avoid things that remind them of that experience. So, every time they see a trigger, they experience panic attacks or flashbacks. This can prevent them from experiencing other things and will eventually isolate them from others.

This type of anxiety disorder should be treated as soon as possible to relieve your psychological distress and avoid any long-term damaging effects. Symptoms of post-traumatic stress disorder include recurring memories of a specific traumatic experience, constant nightmares about it, and terrifying negative thoughts related to it. Along with this, people with PTSD also experience rapid heart rates, profuse sweating, anxiety, and sometimes emotional numbness.

One of the best treatments recommended by therapists is cognitive-behavioral therapy. CBT helps people overcome trauma and eliminate negative thoughts about that scenario and replace them with positive ones that can help them sleep better at night. It can also change how they react to a particular object, situation, or person that could trigger their PTSD. Trauma-focused CBT can use a variety of techniques that will help people triumph over this mental disorder and find other, healthier, and more positive outlets to direct their energy.

Overcoming Anxiety

Most anxiety is caused because your thoughts are either fixated on bad events from the past or else focused too much on the future. You can do a lot to help your anxiety by grounding your thoughts in the present only. By focusing on the present, you stop dwelling on things that you can't change in the past and you stop worrying about things that may never even happen in the future.

But if fixating on the past or present is a habit of yours, you may wonder how you can ground yourself in the present more. Thinking in the present is certainly a healthy habit that will take some mental effort to achieve. One thing that can help you is trying mindfulness.

There is another huge benefit to mindfulness. Mindfulness makes you aware of your thoughts. That enables you to control them better, which helps you overcome and break poor mental habits. Mindfulness is really just the habit of being totally aware of your current existence. You maintain awareness of what is going on around you and what is going on in your mind. This may sound relatively simple, but if you think about it, you spend a lot of time with your mind drifting away from your present surroundings and you probably have very little consciousness or control over your thoughts until they enter your mind, seemingly out of the blue. You are more preoccupied with your worries, plans, and daydreams than your current existence. Therefore, becoming mindful can be a bit of a challenge. It is a new form of awareness and a new style of thinking that you must develop. Essentially, it is an important skill that you must master.

It is also helpful to think about times in your life when you are truly mindful without trying. There are probably some moments when you get so into what is presently happening that you shut out all worries and other distractions. Sex, fun, and deep conversation are examples of times when you might become mindful. Now, imagine reliving those moments right now. Try to capture that feeling again and apply it to your current situation. Try to feel that way all over again. The more you relive that feeling of being mindful in your memory, the more your mind will get used to the sensation. Soon, the state of being mindful will become more normal to your mind. You will be able to achieve the feeling and the focus instantly, at will.

Love can help encourage you to be mindful, as well. When you are engaged in an activity that brings you true enjoyment, you find that you are willing to become absorbed in the activity. You need to do things that you enjoy, anyway. This adds zest to your life and gives you a reason to keep moving forward in life. Take some time for yourself and do something that you really love. It does not matter what it is, as long as it is not something harmful, like taking drugs or hurting yourself in any other way. Healthy, meaningful activities are what keep you sane and add joy to your days. You are miserable enough with your anxiety and depression; why deprive yourself of fun activities and things that you genuinely enjoy?

It can be hard to clear time in your schedule to practice mindfulness. But you must practice it. Just a few minutes a day is sufficient to get some practice in. When you are about to go to bed is a great time to engage in lengthier meditations. You will find that practicing mindfulness meditation before bed will help you sleep more soundly because it helps you turn off your restless brain and just focus on relaxation. A quiet mind is what you need for sleep, but often anxiety prevents you from achieving that level of mental quietness. I do not recommend trying to use physical activity for mindfulness right before bed, however, as this will only increase your energy level and heart rate, making sleep harder. Calming exercise like yoga or Tai Chi can be great before bed, but only if you practice a routine designed for bringing about sleep.

Chapter 6:
Using CBT to Beat OCD
and Intrusive Thoughts

It is a given fact that all people experience unwanted intrusive thoughts. These are not limited to people who have been diagnosed with OCD, and intrusive thoughts are not just negative but can also be positive. So, the truth of the matter is, we can never be free from unwanted intrusive thoughts.

So, in overcoming OCD, the focus must be given to our physical and emotional responses to these thoughts. We must try to achieve not having anxiety or any type of mental or physical compulsion once faced with these thoughts.

With the proper treatment and support, the challenge of achieving this is minimized. Most people do recover from OCD without it ever coming back. Now let's look at several CBT strategies that can aid in alleviating and treating obsessive thoughts:

Habit Reversal Training

Habit Reversal Training or HRT is one of the most commonly used types of behavioral therapy in treating OCD. It reverses the habits formed by individuals that are typically performed in certain situations and help them overcome the urge to do it. This is also helpful in treating different behaviors caused by a variety of conditions, like Tourette's Syndrome.

HRT is seen to be highly effective in helping people with unwanted behaviors or habits, such as hair pulling, tics, repetitive behaviors, or nail-biting. When treating OCD, it is highly recommended to use this type of behavioral therapy since it helps them get rid of the urge to follow the compulsion and minimize or possibly stop their repetitive behavior. This training is made up of five different parts that can help individuals overcome their disorder. It starts with:

Awareness Training

If you want to minimize or put an end to your behavior, it is important to recognize and accept it beforehand. How can you put an end to something if you are not aware of it? The same goes with this; you can't stop your behavior if you aren't even aware of its presence. Through awareness training, individuals pay attention to their behavior and work at diminishing it. This step allows you to figure out when you typically perform this particular behavior, and what are some triggers and signs before you actually do it are. Awareness training helps individuals know and understand their behavior more deeply and find out things they never knew before.

Identifying and Strategizing

This step identifies the problem in your behavior and partly continues the work done in the first step. Once you've identified all the triggers and urges you have, it is time to strategize new behavior or a way to combat your urge. This new behavior will replace the old one. It is important to practice this new behavior and become aware of it. Whenever you want to go back to the old behavior you have been so used to, you can try to do this instead. For example, if your typical behavior in response to nerve-racking situations is biting your nails, the new behavior you'll have to do is to purse your lips instead.

Finding Your Own Motivation and Sticking With Your Plan

When doing something difficult, we tend to find a source of motivation to keep us going or to remind us why we're here in the first place. The same goes with Habit Reversal Therapy; there will be some instances where you'll question what you're doing or why you're even doing it in the first place. This is why you need to write down a list of all the reasons you want to go through HRT and make this a source of your motivation. Find all the people you want to do this for and all the problems you've had because of your unwanted behavior. After finding your motivation, it is important to stick with your HRT and try to comply with it until the very end.

Reducing and Relaxing

These unwanted behaviors tend to show up whenever a person's body is put under a great amount of stress. So, it is important to reduce your stress level and eliminate any triggers that may induce your tics. Relax your body more and give it enough time to rest. In this part, it is important to know different relaxation techniques. Some also coincide with CBT techniques such as deep breathing exercises, progressive muscle relaxation, mindfulness meditation, and the like.

Testing and Training

After all the different processes you've gone through, it's time to test out and practice your new skills and behavior and see how you respond to different situations. You may be placed in front of triggers, and it is important to train yourself to get rid of the urge to go back to your old habits. This is the most crucial step of all because it displays all the work you've done in the past. Once you've practiced this new behavior enough, it will soon become an automatic response for you, successfully replacing the old behavior you once had.

These steps can help individuals overcome their unwanted tics. With a little effort and concentration, they can possibly get through and develop new behavioral patterns.

Imaginal Exposure (IE)

OCD is a complex psychological problem. With a lot of different types and subtypes, it can be difficult to determine which treatment is best for each individual. Some treatments require a lot more intensive procedures than others. Let's look at Exposure and Response Therapy, for example. This type of therapy can be applicable for people who have OCD about physical things like getting germs from touching a doorknob. The simple ERT procedure would be to let them touch multiple doorknobs without letting them wash their hands. However, it cannot apply to individuals who have more complex OCD behaviors. For example, individuals who are afraid of losing loved ones cannot perform ERT. So, as a substitute for this, they can undergo Imaginal Exposure or IE. Through IE, individuals experience visualization of different scenarios that expose them to their fears or OCD. Imaginal Exposure will expose them to seemingly real-life situations and train them on how to react to these particular situations.

Imaginal Exposure is more complex and harder to handle OCD problems. Some opt to go through visualizing different scenarios, while others choose to write imaginal exposure stories. Through visualization, patients are asked to undergo the following process:

- Think of a particular situation that triggers your OCD (like losing the ones you love).

- Once you've identified the situation, start imagining yourself in the scenario (you may be facing it by standing or looking at it).

- Afterward, try to picture that specific scenario over and over again until it does not induce any visible or emotional trigger in you.

After being exposed to it several times, try your best to come back to that scene until you can accept that it isn't reality, and it will not always be like that. This will reduce your negative emotions and change your behavior towards different circumstances.

Through visualization, individuals can easily access their minds and visualize their OCD triggers. By confronting their worst fears, they can slowly reduce their level of anxiety and the intensity of their emotions.

There is also another way to use Imaginal Exposure, and that is through writing imaginative stories. These stories entail your greatest fear, and through them, you find a way to confront these emotions. Through writing your fears, you can let out everything you feel and expose yourself to the different OCD triggers within you. This short story will write will consist of your obsessive thoughts taken to the worst-case scenario. Individuals with OCD may not be too keen to begin or go through this type of therapy. However, it can be very crucial in allowing them to overcome their greatest fears and face their negative thoughts once and for all.

Here are some tips on how to write your own imaginal exposure short story to get the best results and to really impact your thoughts, emotions, and behaviors:

Make Your Story From Your Perspective

As you are trying to overcome your own fear, it is important to write things from a first-person point of view. This is so that we will actually feel the things we "did" in the story and keep it as close to our hearts as possible. This will allow you to see the consequences of your actions and actually feel the story. In the cognitive aspect, the brain will process the information as if it was your own doing, therefore making the therapy effective.

Always Keep It Realistic

It is important not to go beyond the bar. There is a fine line between reality and imagination, so you mustn't go beyond that line. Keep things around the aspects that you think may happen if ever you did a certain act. Don't go far from the actual topic and try to keep things as realistic as possible.

Use Authenticity

Be authentic about the thoughts you're currently thinking about and the emotions you're currently feeling. Only talk about the things that are bothering you. If it isn't actually a problem, then don't bother to write about it.

Focus on the Now and Write in the Present Tense

Write your story in the present tense so that you'll feel you're living in it at the exact same moment. Don't go and write about it as if it happened a year ago; write things as if they are fresh and currently happening.

Keep It Concise

When writing, it is important not to beat around the bush. Keep things as short and concise as possible. If it isn't important, then don't bother to write about it. Don't waste your time writing about things that don't actually keep you up at night. Rather, focus on things that detail the most important and vital part of your illness. Of course, for those with a flair for the language, it is alright to give free rein to your creative expression. Just stay on point while doing it.

Go to the Limit

Take your fear of the worst possible scenario. Make it out to be the worst thing that could ever happen to you in your entire life. In this way, you become exposed to the worst things and learn how to cope with situations like this.

Imaginal exposure can be of great use for individuals who cannot undergo ERT. It can also be extremely helpful for OCD since it exposes them to different made-up scenarios that also resemble real-life situations. Through IE, individuals can touch on both their cognitive and behavioral aspects, which will, in turn, produce positive thoughts and better behavior.

Chapter 7:
Using CBT to Beat Procrastination

Many factors can cause us to procrastinate. These factors will be understood and we'll look at the tools CBT has to break this bad habit.

Are You a Procrastinator?

Many factors can influence how procrastinators behave and what tasks they delay. Consider the reasons you may delay doing what you know is necessary. Are you prone to falling into any of these situations due to procrastination?

- Realizing you didn't leave yourself enough time to finish a task by the deadline.

- **Feeling inadequately prepared for meetings.** Try to force yourself to complete a task.

- Stressing about time and rushing to get to appointments.

- You are trying to conceal that you haven't been working on a task.

- You're able to produce lower-quality work.

- **You can tell yourself that you will take care of it sooner.** Waiting until you feel inspired and motivated to complete a task.

- Finding ways to waste time instead of doing what you need to do.

- Relying on last-minute pressure to complete a task.

Let's start by looking at why we procrastinate and then look at ways to overcome it.

What Drives Procrastination?

There have been many times when we were faced with a paper to finish, an errand that needed to be run, a project at home to complete, and many other things. These delays seem to bring little good. Procrastination has been linked with poor academic performance and worse health. We often find it difficult to manage things on time. These are some of the factors that contribute to our procrastination tendencies:

Fear of the Unpleasant

Our minds tend to gravitate towards the least enjoyable parts of a task when we think about it. When we picture cleaning out the gutters, our minds immediately think of climbing up the ladder. Writing a paper is a way to think about the struggles we will face in communicating our ideas clearly.

Negative Reinforcement

When we put off a task, we believe it will be difficult. The brain experiences a sense of relief. That relief is interpreted by the brain as a reward. We are more likely to do the same thing that brought us that reward. This is how procrastination gets reinforced. It is called "negative reinforcement" by psychologists because it removes something that is perceived as aversive. Positive reinforcement, on the other hand, is when we get something we enjoy that strengthens our behavior. For example, a paycheck reinforces our job performance. Negative reinforcement can make it difficult to avoid a task. Are there tasks you have been meaning to do but keep putting off? These are the factors that can contribute to procrastination. Write down all the ways you procrastinate and what causes it. Is procrastination always a bad thing?

Researchers have found that procrastination has many benefits. Procrastination can make it harder to find solutions and help us harness the pressure of a deadline to boost our productivity. Adam Grant, a management professor, wrote about the positive effects of procrastination and creativity. Dr. Grant says that our first ideas are more conventional. If we give ourselves more time, we can come up with better solutions. However, we are less likely to reach the best solution if we rush. These benefits must be balanced against the stress, missed deadlines, and lower quality work that procrastinating can bring.

Strategies to Beat Procrastination

Knowing the causes of procrastination can help us understand how to get out. Procrastination can be caused by multiple factors so we need many tools to help us overcome it. The tools can be broken down into three categories:

1. Think (cognitive)

2. Act (behavioral)

3. Be (mindfulness)

These three areas can be combined to create a strategy that works for you.

Procrastination can be made more likely by certain conditions. Depression can make it difficult to manage our energy and motivation. ADHD sufferers have difficulty meeting deadlines because they are unable to focus on one task and lack the motivation to finish it. Procrastination can also be a result of anxiety disorders, such as procrastination. For example, someone might put off writing an email because they fear saying the wrong thing.

Think: Cognitive Strategies

How we think about the task, and how willing and able to complete it, are two major factors in procrastination. Procrastination can be reduced by strategic changes to our thinking.

- **Recognize that you won't feel like doing it any sooner.** It's easy to assume that we will get to a task when we feel like it. Likely, we won't feel the need to complete it later than we do now. It's not necessary to wait for the perfect moment.

- **Refute the belief that you have to do something "perfectly."** Many people put off starting a task due to unrealistic expectations of how it should be done. It doesn't need to be perfect.

- Write down the Think strategies that you find most appealing in your journal and practice them whenever necessary.

Being on Time

Lateness is a sign of procrastination. It refers to a delay in getting from one place or another within a given time frame. These principles will help you improve your punctuality:

- **Be realistic about how long it will take to reach your destination.** Calculate how long it will take to get there. You should factor in any unexpected delays (e.g., traffic delays) to ensure you don't underestimate how long it takes to reach your destination.

- **To ensure you are on time, be careful when setting your watch or clock ahead.** This strategy can often backfire because we know that our watches are fast and can ignore it.

- **Do not start activity too close to the time you are leaving.** Avoid trying to squeeze in an extra activity before you leave for your destination.

- **In case you are early, bring things to do.** You don't want to be too early, waste your time, and end up feeling anxious.

Chapter 8:
Releasing Regret and Getting Over Guilt Using CBT

You want to move ahead in life and find fulfillment. You cannot see this if you have beliefs that hold you back. To successfully eliminate these limiting beliefs, the following strategies should be of help:

Loudly, Read Out Your Opinion and Ask Yourself if You Know That It Is True

Check if you have experienced it many times to make it right. Keep in mind, concluding limited experiences will not give you the correct answer. Ensure that you have no doubts whatsoever in establishing the belief to be true.

It is not possible for a person without money to tell how to have it and the consequences of having it. You must also establish if the origin of your belief is credible or not. Ideas are developed from personal experiences and expert advice. Rely on information from experts to change your mindset.

Make a simple, bold statement and decide not to believe the belief you hold anymore because it is not valid.

When a person boldly states their intention, and it usually has a great impact on their life. To reinforce that your belief is false, look for evidence that supports this fact, such as:

- Whoever told you that has no experience or knowledge on the subject

- You have relied on other people's experience yet you have never tried it to know

- Against all the odds, others that were more disadvantaged than you have succeeded and you have witnessed it

If you think on those lines, you will begin to doubt the validity of the limiting belief you have held. Research and read more on the subject that you feel your ideas are limiting and see how you can change. Visualize changing your life by eliminating the belief.

Come Up With a New Belief That Is Beneficial

For every limiting belief, come up with an opposite view. Come up with the idea that will improve your life and motivate you to improve your experience. Do this by getting evidence that supports your new positive belief. This helps to create stability for your understanding.

For every new belief, make sure you get evidence to support it to be true.

Evaluate Yourself

With each day, consider performing a proper audit on yourself. Evaluate how you feel about the new belief. How do you think about your opinion? What is your gut instinct regarding the original idea? Do you feel that your behavior is changing?

Be genuine with the response you come up with. If you can change your beliefs, how you behave and feel will change. Each person's life is a manifestation of his or her feelings. When you genuinely change your expectations, you will also be able to transform your life fully.

Keep going back to your list of beliefs and keep changing those that influence negatively your life. As you progress in making the changes, you will discover other limiting beliefs and work on improving them. With each step of your life, you will set new goals that will challenge you differently.

With each new goal you set, evaluate how to get there, the possible obstacles, and what beliefs you have that may limit you from achieving the goals. Make it a habit to continuously evaluate yourself, identify the limiting beliefs, and eliminate them.

Psychology and Spirituality to Change Your Core Beliefs

Psychology is defined as the study of how our mind works and affects our behavior. Psychology as science investigates the causes of actions and can be used to change practices as well.

Spirituality is different from religion. It is about understanding who you are by looking beyond what you see. Spirituality is very central in forming a person's core beliefs.

People's core beliefs affect their outward behavior. Through psychology and spirituality, one can transform their life into what one visualizes. This can be done through a transformation of the mindset.

Most of the issues people encounter are a result of having underlying believes or questions. Both spirituality and psychology look at transforming your thoughts to improve your life.

To change your life, you must begin by completely transforming your mindset. The nature of your thoughts determines the quality of your life. Positive thoughts, optimism, feelings, and emotions generate some form of energy in your system that allows you to have internal joy.

How we act, is a direct manifestation of our thoughts. Psychology and spirituality work together to bring a change in the way a person thinks and generate happiness and fulfillment in our daily lives.

It is possible to change your thoughts and transform your life. Here is a list of ways that you can use to improve your ideas and transform your life positively.

Create Positive Affirmations

Affirmations can also be harmful. Unfortunately, most people are used to making negative affirmations. When a person repeatedly thinks, they are going to fail, it is an example of a negative statement. Both negative and positive affirmations affect the functioning of your brain.

Mantras are examples of positive affirmations. Mantras are almost sacred with a spiritual. When creating positive affirmations, they should not be weak or average.

Examples of negative affirmations are: "I can't be able. It is impossible." On the other side, positive affirmations are determined and forceful like "I can or I will." Your brain responds to how you think and, as such, directs the rest of the body organs to act as per your thoughts.

Know When to Stop

Many people like to dwell on the misfortunes they have encountered along the way. The wrongs they perceive were committed against them by their loved ones. They keep cursing themselves because of the mistakes they made and analyzing what they could have done differently.

It is OK to learn from our past and plan to do better in the future. However, it is not healthy to dwell in the past because we forget to move forward with life.

Stop Being Masochistic

Many times, people want to wallow in self-pity and misery. We create self-punishing thoughts and enjoy that state of mind; we focus on pessimistic thoughts and being consistently gloomy. Some people will believe they are naturally unlucky, and so nothing good will ever happen in their lives.

These kinds of thoughts are harmful to your mind and equally detrimental to your physical health.

Count Your Blessings and Your Joys

Don't take your blessings and joy for granted. Stop grumbling every time you are faced with a challenge. You can counter this by always remembering those that are less fortunate in life than you. It is also possible for a situation to have been worse, think about that too.

Practice gratitude to enjoy the fullness of life. When you are grateful, the negatives turn to positives. Where there is chaos, the order becomes. Where there is confusion, clarity becomes. This is only possible by having a grateful attitude.

Appreciate What You Have

The easiest and most excellent way to transform your thoughts is by enjoying and appreciating what you have. Instead of feeling sad because of what you have not achieved in life yet, try being appreciative of where you are now.

Fixing your eyes on more important things is good. However, to reach those great heights, you must begin where you are and enjoy it. If you don't achieve your goals, appreciate what you have so far, and it will motivate you to make more.

Enjoy Your Achievements

Achieving your goals and enjoying them are two different things. Many people set out with goals in mind. As soon as they make them, they become restless and look for more instead of enjoying what they have achieved. If you aim to achieve something, follow your goals, and once you do, appreciate the effort and achievement.

When Trials Come, Stand Tall

It is natural to feel unmotivated and demoralized when we face challenging conditions. We stop moving and focus on exploring the weight of the challenges. However, try and lift your spirits, and you will feel better.

Hold your head high and, with determination, face the challenges to get out of them successfully.

Enjoy the Child in You

Children are pure in their thinking and innocent. They will fight or quarrel with their friends and forget it so fast and start playing together once again. Unfortunately for grownups, we hold issues within us that poison our spirit and minds. As children, it is essential to practice forgiving and to forget an incident as soon as it has happened and talked over.

Seek to Be Happy and Contented

Most people associate their happiness with events in the future. They peg their happiness to future happenings, and if those things don't happen, they are no longer happy. Don't postpone your joy; instead, enjoy your moment today because tomorrow does not belong to you.

Control Your Moods

Don't be a servant to your moods; instead, be the master. Remember, you define your happiness. Never allow circumstances or people to dampen your spirit and make you unhappy.

Other people associate their happiness with material possessions; do not attach your pleasure to things. Choose to be happy, regardless of the situation. Don't allow heartbreaks to dominate; you instead find joy under all circumstances.

Resolve to Have a Happy Day

Every day comes with challenges and situations that can trigger unhappiness. Wake up every day with a determination to be happy. Identify things that bring you joy and focus on those. Look to nature for inspiration and joy.

Purpose to stay calm despite the situations you may face and remain happy.

Honor Your Body Because It Is Your Temple

Consider your Body to be sacred. Keep it well cleaned and avoid dumping garbage, toxic food, and negative thoughts in it. To stay happy, you must stay healthy, both mentally and physically. Engage in active physical exercises often and read inspiring content that acts to motivate you.

Learn to Meditate Daily

Meditation does not have to be complicated, as some people have made it be. Every evening, find a quiet place, focus on how your day was, and pay attention to the good things that made you feel good. If something not so pleasant happened, focus on the lessons you learned from the situation but do not attract negative thoughts by regretting it. By doing this, you fill your mind with gratitude and create a happier you.

Forget About Changing the World but Focus on Improving Yourself

When people fall short of your expectations, do not get upset. You cannot change the world, but the best way is to change how you view the world by changing yourself. By changing yourself, you allow yourself to adjust to the situations around you, and in so doing, you avoid stress.

Use What You Have and Make the Best of It

Do not focus your energies on thinking of what the best could be. Instead, take what you have and make the best out of it. The world is not ideal. Forget the imperfections around you. Change your thoughts and change your world.

Thoughts are compelling. Your ideas can be an obstacle to your happiness or the cause of your mental health issues. You are transforming your thoughts results in the transformation of your mindset. When your mind is changed, you live a healthier, happier, and more fulfilling life.

Cognitive-behavioral therapy focuses on transforming your mindset from a negative one to a positive one. Identifying your core beliefs and how they affect your thought pattern is the beginning of your transformation.

Chapter 9:
How CBT Can Help You Beat Addiction

Addiction ruins life. It prevents people from forming and maintaining relationships, being productive at work and/or school, and functioning normally in society. So, before it becomes too late, you should find ways on how to prevent yourself from being addicted to illegal drugs, alcohol, and other things.

One way to prevent addiction is through intervention and screening. Prevention has to start in childhood and continue in adolescence. This way, addiction can be successfully prevented in adulthood.

Strategies for Preventing Addictions

There is a variety of strategies you can use to prevent addictions. These strategies should be employed to help old and young people understand the implications of using illegal substances and prevent them from making a negative impact on their lives.

In schools and communities, for example, addiction can be prevented by teaching children and adolescents to resist social pressure. They should be taught that they do not have to go along with their peers to belong. They can be independent and still make friends. They should also be taught how to improve their self-esteem, manage their anxiety and stress, and improve their communication and decision-making skills.

Taxes should also be increased for alcohol and tobacco products. In addition, the availability of excess prescription medications should be reduced. Advertisements and marketing of addictive substances should be restricted as well.

Self-Help Tips on How to Prevent Addictions

For the past years, researchers have tried to discover what causes people to develop addictions to substances or behaviors. They have found that all addictions trigger a neurological response that activates the reward system in the brain. This causes an addicted individual to crave more of his addiction.

Sadly, certain things can never be changed when preventing addiction. These include family history, past trauma, and childhood environment. All of these factors contribute to the way a person thinks, feels, and behaves. They also contribute to their anxiety, depression, and addiction.

Fortunately, there are still plenty of ways on how you can deal with your anxiety, stress, or depression. Likewise, there are still lots of ways on how you can prevent addiction. Here are some of them:

Deal With Past Trauma and Pain

If your past is haunting or bothering you in the present, you have to face it and deal with it head-on. Ignoring or repressing it will only make your condition worse. You need to deal with whatever is coming back from the past to mess with your present. Read self-help books and attend support groups. If necessary, you should work with a therapist to help you deal with past trauma and hurts.

Seek Help From Professionals

If you are impulsive, lack self-control, are antisocial, or are aggressive, you should seek professional assistance. The National Institute on Drug Abuse recommends working with a therapist to help you deal with drug or alcohol abuse. You can also speak with a counselor regarding your intense sensations and extreme experiences.

Surround Yourself With Supportive People

You can get better faster if you have adequate support from your loved ones, mental health professionals, and other people. This is especially true if you are part of the lesbian, gay, bisexual, transgender, or queer (LGBTQ) community. According to the Centers for Disease Control, the members of this community are more likely to use and abuse drugs or alcohol. They turn to these substances in an attempt to deal with their self-esteem issues, trauma, and other problems.

Choose Your Friends Wisely

Peer pressure is present at any age. Even adults can be pressured into doing something. So, if you want to prevent addictions, you should refrain from hanging out with people who have them. This way, you can avoid being exposed to addictive substances as well as being encouraged to use them.

Do Not Start Young

People who start using illegal substances or drinking at an early age are more likely to develop addictions later in life. If you have children or relatives who are teenagers, tell them to avoid using these substances and remind them of the consequences of using them. Spread the word about addiction to help more people avoid it.

Learn About the Consequences of Addiction

You may not realize the consequences of your actions. Once you do, however, you may have a change of heart. Once you find out what happens to your mind and body as well as how your addiction can affect your loved ones, you may be motivated to change your ways.

Form Strong Connections

Sometimes, all you need are people who care about you. You may just need a friend to talk to about your woes. Once you develop friendships, you may no longer feel the need to turn to drugs or alcohol to drown your sorrows. When you have people who support and listen to you, you can feel more at peace.

Take Part in Anti-Drug, Alcohol, and Tobacco Programs in Your Community

According to researchers, these programs are effective in helping people change their ways and maintain their new lifestyles. These early intervention programs can help people prevent risky behaviors.

Determine Your Personal Triggers

Everyone's triggers are different. For some individuals, getting drunk or high is the direct result of anxiety or stress. For others, it is the result of hanging out with friends who like to drink at bars.

In order to determine your personal triggers, you have to ask yourself when you think about alcohol or drugs the most. Find out which situations make you more likely to use and abuse these substances. Identify what your reasons are for using them. Do you use them to momentarily forget about pain or responsibilities? Do you use them to release stress?

Once you get the answers to these questions, you should plan a way to work on them. You have to determine trigger situations when they occur so that you can take the necessary steps to stay away from them.

Avoid Stress

Stress is one of the most common reasons why people turn to alcohol, nicotine, and illegal drugs. They say that they just want to release stress.

So, if you want to prevent addictions, you should avoid getting stressed in the first place. To avoid it, you can practice breathing exercises. Close your eyes and take deep breaths. You can also distract yourself by engaging in enjoyable activities. You can also turn to exercise to release feel-good chemicals in your body and feel better immediately.

A mind that has been ruined by drug addiction is the perfect breeding ground for negative thoughts and other emotional health issues. Managing challenging thoughts and emotions is hard enough for a sober person, but the experience is ten times worse when you consider a drug addict. Thankfully, drug addicts can benefit from CBT. Cognitive-behavioral therapy has been shown to achieve long-lasting results in the treatment of various addiction types.

Benefits of CBT in Addiction Treatment

Provides a Network of Support

Cognitive-behavioral therapy allows addicts to have a network of support, which is very crucial during the recovery phase. The average addict, if not given positive encouragement, could easily relapse into drug abuse. Therapists are there to offer positive encouragement and gently guide these people toward full healing. When addicts realize that no one cares about them, they are likely to go back to seek solace from drugs. Having a network of support is critical for avoiding relapse and ensuring general emotional well-being. People are social beings. Thanks to the support network, addicts have someone to talk to.

Increased Positive Thought Patterns

Addicts often struggle with a negative thought pattern that makes them feel helpless, ultimately making them go back to doing drugs. An addict struggles with many bleak thoughts and feelings. However, through the power of positivity, they can overcome their mental and emotional health issues. CBT emphasizes positivity. The more positive an individual is, the less likely they are to slide back into drug addiction. Therapists help addicts overcome their conditions by planting positive thoughts in their subconscious. This helps addicts become positive by default. And whenever they experience emotional troubles, they have someone to guide them.

Enhancement of Self-Esteem

Low self-esteem is one of the reasons why people turn to drugs and alcohol. They want to forget their misery and helplessness. But cognitive behavioral therapy helps addicts develop a great self-image. As their self-esteem level goes up, they find less desire to escape reality through drugs and alcohol. They are happy to be themselves. Therapists constantly reinforce addicts' self-esteem and thus raise their desire wanting a better life than the one they presently have. To get rid of an addiction, the affected person must want to change their circumstances, and this desire becomes natural when an addict's self-esteem is given a boost.

Learning to Resist Peer Pressure

Since we are social beings seeking peer acceptance, it is exceptionally challenging to resist peer pressure. It is challenging for the average person, and ten times more challenging for the drug addict. Cognitive-behavioral therapy equips addicts with the skills for overcoming peer pressure and focusing on their important life goals. When it comes to resisting peer pressure, they are trained first to imagine saying "no" to their peers, and then actually saying "no" within a controlled environment. By the end of the training, they won't have any difficulty saying "no" to both their peers and anyone else who might negatively influence them.

Cost-Effectiveness

Cognitive-behavioral therapy is one of the most affordable addiction treatment methods. Some other treatment methods, like rehabs, have in-house arrangements for the patient. These treatment methods can be incredibly expensive. Cognitive-behavioral therapy can be conducted on an outpatient basis and achieve great results. Insurance plans even cover this treatment method. Cognitive-behavioral therapy is not one-sided. For its success, both the therapist and the patient must work side by side. If the patient is not cooperative, then the treatment will tumble down. Cognitive-behavioral therapy is not complicated. It involves general procedures that lead to the restoration of health. There are no expensive or complicated tools required.

Gradual Steps

Overcoming an addiction is no walk in the park. It is a time-consuming quest. Remedies that claim to offer instant results are misleading. In cognitive-behavioral therapy, a therapist introduces new principles to the patient as they advance through the treatment. There are principles set aside for beginners and principles set aside for those who have reached the advanced stage. Walking through these steps, the patient's resolve is strengthened, and they are less likely to run back to drugs or alcohol than patients who have been through any other treatment model. The beauty of cognitive behavioral therapy is that it doesn't advertise itself as a quick fix. It takes real effort to achieve results. However, the effects are long-lasting.

Continuity of Normal Activities

Cognitive-behavioral therapy is done in an outpatient arrangement. The patient is free to indulge in other activities for the rest of their time. This is unlike rehabs, where patients are held on campus, effectively suspending their daily engagements such as going to work. With cognitive behavioral therapy, patients are neither separated from their family nor do they have to seek leave. Because of its flexibility, more people are willing to take this treatment method. And if the sessions are scheduled at night, then your day will run without even a slight hitch.

Gradual End to Therapy

Cognitive-behavioral therapy places the entire focus on the patient. The concepts and exercises may be adjusted following how the patient is faring. In some forms of addiction therapy, the treatment lasts only for a specific time, and then it is cut off. This kind of arrangement doesn't take care of patients who would take ordinarily long to recover fully. In cognitive-behavioral therapy, the first few weeks are typically intensive. Still, as the patient's condition improves, the therapist finds less need to have intensive sessions and focuses on the patient's recovery speed.

Chapter 10:
Using CBT to Overcome Jealousy

Finding jealousy is similar to changing any mental or behavioral response. It all starts with consciousness. The ability to see the truth of your own thoughts and feelings allows you to recognize that they aren't real. You will stop responding to the possibilities that your imagination may create if you are so simple. Anger and jealousy are emotions that you may not believe are true. These negative emotional reactions can be changed by changing how you think. Even if you feel justified, envy and anger are not ways to deal with the situation and achieve what we want. You can't change your anxiety or resentment if you feel like you are trying to control a car sliding on ice. Clearing the risk is a good way to improve your ability to handle the situation. It is important to address the causes of jealousy, rather than try to control your emotions. Permanently ending a relationship means changing your unconscious expectations and fears about the actions of your partner.

The Steps to End Jealous Reactions Permanently

You can regain your personal power and control your emotions to stop reacting. Identify the core beliefs that trigger the emotional response. Your convictions may not be valid. This is different from "knowing" scientifically that the claims are false. You can gain control over your focus to actively select your mind's storyline and emotions. The envy dynamic is influenced by many factors. Practical solutions will address multiple elements such as values, emotions, feelings, and personal will. If you are lacking one or more of these elements, you will be able to exhibit negative emotions and behavior.

It is possible to step back and not react emotionally by doing some simple exercises. If you are looking to improve your emotions and behavior, this is possible. You just need to be willing to learn the skills.

Principle Triggers of Jealousy Are Convictions Which Create Insecurity Feelings

Low self-esteem can be attributed to a lack of belief in who you are. We don't have to abandon our false self-image to eliminate fear and low self-esteem. Although this might seem difficult for some, most people don't have the skills to change their beliefs. It takes little effort to change a belief if you put in the work. It is as simple as stopping thinking about the story. Believe it takes more effort than believing something.

Self-Judgment May Intensify the Feeling of Insecurity

It's not enough to intellectually "learn" emotion. Only then will the Inner Judge be able to abuse us by criticizing what we do. This knowledge could be used by the Interior Judge to make us more vulnerable and push us into an emotional downward spiral. You will need to learn skills to dispel false self-images, beliefs, and control your mind projects. You can access the practices and skills from the audio sessions. The first and second sessions of the audio sessions are free. They should provide an overview of the mind's ability to create emotions. Sessions 1 and 2 provide great exercises that will help you regain your personal power and adjust to your emotions.

To change behavior, one must first understand how jealousy or wrath is created in our minds. This step allows us to take control and put us in a position where we can change our emotions.

If you are in a jealous relationship and wish to change your behavior, we won't accept responsibility. You could say things like "When you wouldn't, I wouldn't respond like that." This language indicates a weak attitude. It attempts to control your behavior through dealing with it.

How Does the Mind Produce the Emotions of Anger and Jealousy?

In the following description, I describe the mechanisms of anger and jealousy. You probably already understand the complexities of envy and how to overcome it. This explanation may help you to understand how the mind transforms knowledge into self-judgment, which can lead to low self-esteem or insecurity. This theoretical understanding can help you to develop consciousness to see the complexities of life. To make major changes, you will need to have a new set of skills. It is not clear enough how your emotions are formed. It's like discovering you have a flat-tired car. You didn't know what to do because you stumbled across the screw.

Compensating for Fear

He focuses on his positive qualities to overcome the negative emotion he feels from his hidden false image. These attributes create a positive False Image of the man. This is the Projected Picture. He needs to be seen as this. A positive self-image does not lead to self-rejection and indignity. He is more accepting and generates more love, happiness, and joy. He hasn't changed, but he may have a different picture depending on the moment.

The belief in a hidden image can cause unhappiness while the projection image creates more positive emotions. Both images are fake, it is important to remember. Both images exist in the mind and are not his. He creates the images and then reacts to them in his imagination. He is not an image in his imagination.

The man's mind combines the image projected with the characteristics that women are attracted to. These characteristics are often deemed positive as women love them. A man who is attracted to a woman's image will link himself to it instead of thinking he is not good enough. Increased trust in the projected picture leads to greater social acceptance, love, happiness, and even romance.

Chapter 11:
Becoming More Assertive and Coping With Criticism

In a healthy relationship, both people can talk about their needs, and they can give and receive constructive criticism without feeling threatened or rejected.

Unfortunately, many of us aren't very good at telling our partners when we would like to change something in our relationship. We might worry that they will resent us, or maybe we just don't know how to start a conversation without getting whiny or angry.

What's more, we may find it hard to process criticism, even if it's loving and carefully worded. Anything other than acceptance and praise can feel like a major threat.

This is where assertiveness training comes in. When you behave assertively, you stand up for your wants and needs while respecting your partner and the relationship. But assertiveness goes beyond behavior. It's about adopting a specific mindset that will help you communicate with anyone and develop healthy relationships based on mutual respect.

Here, you'll discover how to stand up for yourself and assert your rights in a relationship. You'll also discover how to handle criticism so you can learn and grow from feedback.

What Does It Mean to Be Assertive?

To understand what assertive behavior is, you can compare and contrast it with passive, aggressive, and passive-aggressive behavior:

Passive Behavior

Passive people put others' needs before their own. They do what they are told. When someone tells them that their needs or opinions are wrong, passive people don't fight back.

When passive people receive criticism, they automatically agree and change their behavior in an attempt to please the other person. They rarely stop to consider whether the feedback is helpful or true. In fact, most passive people tend to have low self-esteem, and so they agree with anyone who says they have messed up, or even that they are a terrible person.

Here are some typical beliefs you might have if you're a passive communicator:

- "Other people know more than I do, so I should listen to them."

- "If someone criticizes me, it means I am a bad person."

- "My ideas and thoughts are probably wrong, so I shouldn't share them."

- "It's arrogant and rude to stand up for your own needs."

Aggressive Behavior

Aggressive people believe that their desires should come first. If they believe someone is trying to get in the way of their wants or needs, they will lash out. Aggressive people aren't always violent. They may use verbal aggression instead or launch a campaign of emotional abuse.

When an aggressive person is criticized, they either dismiss the feedback immediately or become angry. They see criticism as an insult and a threat to their ego.

Here are some typical beliefs you might have if you're an aggressive communicator:

- "Other people should listen to me because my opinions and needs are more important than theirs."

- "Being angry is the only way to get respect."

- "Attack is the best form of defense."

- "As long as I protect myself, it doesn't matter what other people think."

Passive-Aggressive Behavior

Passive-aggressive people may appear compliant on the surface, but their behavior makes it clear that they aren't happy with the situation. They might resort to sabotage as a form of revenge, or just to make it clear how unhappy they are. For instance, a passive-aggressive person might agree to take on a task they don't want to do, but then do such a bad job that no one asks them to do it again.

A passive-aggressive person may not agree when someone criticizes them. If they don't agree with a piece of criticism, they might say so—but in a sarcastic, snide, or subtly dismissive way. Alternatively, they might appear to agree with a piece of critical feedback, but then deliberately ignore it.

Here are some typical beliefs you might have if you're a passive-aggressive communicator:

- "Confrontation is bad, so I have to use sneaky tactics to get my own way."

- "It's unsafe to stand up for myself."

- "Other people can't be trusted."

- "Other people can't tell me what to do."

Assertive Behavior

An assertive person tries to balance their needs with those of others. They know they won't always get what they want, but they believe in standing up for their rights. They make themselves heard, without resorting to intimidation tactics.

When an assertive person receives criticism or negative feedback, they evaluate whether it's true or helpful before responding. They may or may not act on criticism, depending on the source and whether they think it's true. Either way, assertive people have robust self-esteem that can't be damaged by negative feedback.

Here are some typical beliefs you might have if you're an assertive communicator:

- "I'm important and worthy in my own right—and so is everyone else."

- "I can handle difficult conversations."

- "My self-worth doesn't depend on what anyone else thinks."

- "If someone hurts me, I can get over it. I'm strong."

So, how can you become more assertive? First, you need to identify any mental blocks you might have about asserting your rights. Second, you need to master some practical techniques that will rapidly improve your communication skills.

Exercise: What Kind of Communicator Are You?

Based on the descriptions above, how would you describe your communication style? Some of us are a mix of two styles. You might use different styles depending on who you're talking to. For example, you might find it easy to be assertive at work but slip into a passive communication style when arguing with your partner.

Challenge Your Beliefs About Assertiveness

How do you feel when you picture yourself as an assertive person? Nervous, hypocritical, anxious? Lots of us carry around unhelpful beliefs about what it means to be assertive. Unless you take a close look at these beliefs, it will be hard to make progress.

Here are a few of the most common negative beliefs, along with more helpful alternative thoughts:

1. **Belief:** "Being assertive means being a bully."

   Alternative thought: "Bullies are not assertive, they are aggressive. Being assertive is about striking the right balance between standing up for your own rights and respecting other peoples' wishes."

2. **Belief:** "If I'm assertive, I'll drive everyone away."

Alternative thought: "Confident, friendly people will respect me if I'm assertive."

3. **Belief:** "It's not very ladylike to be assertive."

Alternative thought: "Women and girls are taught from an early age that it's unfeminine to be assertive, but it's actually good to be an assertive woman. Assertive women get what they need and want in life."

4. **Belief:** "It's OK for others to be assertive, but my own needs don't matter."

Alternative thought: "Everyone has basic needs. Everyone has the right to be heard and to be respected. That includes me."

5. **Belief:** "Unless I take a 'tough love' approach with others, they won't respect me. They'll walk all over me."

Alternative thought: "Assertive people are usually more respected than angry, aggressive people. True, being aggressive might help me get my own way, but it will damage my relationships. Assertive communication is just as effective—and everyone else will probably like me more, not less."

Practical Tips to Become More Assertive

Start Saying "No" More Often

Are you a people-pleaser? Do you tend to go along with what everyone else wants, only to feel resentful later? The only solution is to learn how to decline requests and invitations. For example, let's suppose your sister wants you to babysit her children on Friday, even though you know you'll be tired at the end of the working week.

Instead of gritting your teeth and saying "Yes," you could use one of the following assertive responses instead:

- "No, I can't, I'll be too tired. I hope you find another solution."

- "Thank you for asking me. You know I like spending time with your kids. But I've got to say 'No' this time because I'll be too tired."

- "No, I'm not available that night."

Practice by saying "No" to low-level requests. For example, if your friend asks you to lend them a small amount of money, you could say, "No, I can't do that. I need to save whatever I can." "No" is a complete answer in its own right. If someone doesn't respect a "No," that's not your fault—they need to learn to respect other peoples' boundaries.

Use "I" Statements

"You" statements can sound accusatory, which isn't helpful if you are in a tense situation. Try to start sentences with "I need," "I feel," or "I would like" instead.

Keep statements simple and to the point. For example:

- "I need to leave by 6 o'clock."

- "This will cost $1,200."

These are examples of "simple assertion." "I" statements are also useful for explaining how you feel. For example:

- "I feel angry."

- "I feel worried."

You can extend "I" statements to show empathy with someone else's position while still asserting your own needs.

For example:

- "I understand that you don't like having dinner earlier in the evening, but until I get settled into my new job, I'd like you to accept that this is the routine for the foreseeable future."

- "I know that you don't like taking phone calls in the evening, but I'd like to get your feedback on an urgent matter."

Watch Your Body Language

Your posture and voice make a big difference in how you feel about yourself, and how others see you. Keep your arms and legs uncrossed, sit or stand up straight, and keep your shoulders relaxed. Keep your tone of voice even. Never shout. If you appear calm and assertive, others will take you more seriously.

Use the Broken Record Technique When Someone Tries to Override You

If someone tries to overload you with objections and irrelevant arguments, rephrase and repeat your original response. Persistent people may ask you the same question several times, but even the rudest individuals will get the message eventually if you stand by your answer. Don't allow yourself to be sidetracked.

Find an Assertiveness Role Model

CBT therapists sometimes tell their clients to find a role model if they are trying to change their behavior. Do you know someone assertive without being aggressive? Watch them carefully and see what you can learn.

Focus on Behavior, Not Character, When Asking Someone to Behave Differently

If you want to ask someone else to change their behavior, use this formula:

- State their observable behavior.

- Tell them how it affects you.

- Tell them how this makes you feel.

- Tell them how you would prefer them to act in the future.

Here's an example of the formula in action:

"When you don't pick up ingredients for dinner on your way home when you promise to do so, it means I have to go and get them myself, come home, then make the evening meal.

This makes me feel tired and disrespected. In the future, I'd like you to either pick up the ingredients or let me know in plenty of time if it won't be possible."

Spell Out Consequences

If you have tried asking someone to change their behavior but to no avail, the next step is to assert consequences. This is only appropriate as a last resort, and only when you are in a position to impose punishments or sanctions. Never make empty threats; the other person may see through them or decide to call your bluff.

Stay calm, keep to the point, and remain civil.

For example:

- "By failing to sign in when you arrive at work for the third time this week, you are violating an important company protocol. If you do this again, I will have to initiate a formal disciplinary procedure."

- "I have asked you to tidy your bedroom, and you have not done it. If you don't do it by tomorrow, I will confiscate your phone over the weekend."

You Have the Right to Put Your Safety First

Don't force yourself to be assertive if doing so would be unsafe. If someone is behaving in an abusive way, or you have a good reason to think they will become very angry if you assert yourself, it's best to excuse yourself from the situation as soon as possible.

Exercise: Role Playing

Role-plays are a safe, effective way to practice your assertiveness skills. Ask someone you trust to play the role of someone who tends to make unreasonable requests. Repeat the role-play several times until you feel confident that you could say "No" in real life. You may wish to start by thinking of a recent example of a time you had trouble declining a request. Re-enact the scene. What could you have done differently?

How to Handle Criticism

No one is perfect. We all receive criticism from time to time. It isn't much fun to hear someone highlight your shortcomings, but criticism can be helpful. If you can accept feedback and act on it, you'll make more progress in your career, studies, and even personal life than people who block out criticism or become overly defensive.

Exercise: How Do You Normally Deal With Criticism?

When was the last time someone criticized you? Did you make the most of the feedback by changing your behavior, or did you try to block it out? Take a moment to think about how your response to criticism might be holding you back from fulfilling your potential.

8 Steps to Handling Criticism

1. **Remind yourself that criticism doesn't determine your self-worth.** You are a valuable and worthy human being, regardless of what anyone may say about you. Even if you have made a mistake, this doesn't mean you are a bad person. When you

remember this, criticism won't seem quite so threatening.

2. **Take a deep breath and wait a moment before reacting.** Give yourself a moment to process what the other person has said. It's better to pause for a few moments, or even to take a few minutes alone, than say or do something you regret.

3. **Consider the source.** Not all criticism is created equal. Do not assume that it is true or justified. Feedback can be completely accurate and fair, or total nonsense. Most of the time, it's somewhere in between. Avoid "all or nothing" thinking. Be prepared to take to heart the criticism that makes sense and dismiss the rest if it's irrelevant or given out of spite.

Talk to a person you trust if you find it hard to differentiate between constructive and destructive criticism. They will be able to help you take a step back and assess the situation.

4. **Ask clarifying questions if the other person is being vague.** If someone gives you a piece of general negative feedback, ask for more information. Some people are not good at communicating what they mean, so you have to put some effort into finding out what they are trying to say.

For example, if someone tells you, "I suppose you'll find it hard to complete this project because you aren't very organized," ask them, "In what ways do you think I'm not very organized?"

5. **Try to focus on the words, not the tone.** Some people lack self-awareness and communication skills and may not know how to keep their tone of voice steady. Keep your focus on what they are saying, not how they are saying it.

6. **Defuse the criticism if it's destructive, inaccurate, or unfair.** You can agree with criticism in part, agree in principle, or agree in probability. The best option depends on the situation and the other person's temperament, but all three techniques work in the same way. They take the sting out of the criticism and lessen the other person's hold on you.

   First, you can agree in part. If the criticism is partly correct, pick out the relevant details and repeat them back to the other person. This lets you defuse the situation without validating the rest of their feedback.

   a. **Criticism:** "You're lazy. You never help around the house, you didn't pick up the dry cleaning, and you hardly ever walk the dog."

   Response: "You're right in saying that I do rarely walk the dog."

   Alternatively, if the other person's logic is correct but their criticism is flawed, you could agree in principle.

   b. **Criticism:** "You aren't using the right software for compiling this report. It has lots of security bugs. We'll lose our most important data."

   Response: "True, if there are security bugs then we could lose some data."

Finally, you agree on probability. This involves acknowledging that, in theory, something could come to pass. However, it doesn't mean you have to agree with the criticism in its entirety.

    c. **Criticism:** "If you don't start keeping to a strict budget, you won't be able to meet your basic expenses. You'll be broke by next year."

    Response: "You're right, I could run out of money."

7. **Apologize if necessary.** If you have made a mistake, own up to it. Make apologies or amends as appropriate.

8. **Decide on an action plan and share it if appropriate.** If the criticism is fair, explain what you will do differently in the future. Be specific. For instance, if your boss has criticized your public speaking ability, you could tell them about the speaking course you intend to take.

Finally, reward yourself! As you've probably noticed, not many people are good at working with criticism. If you can master this skill, your performance at work will improve, you'll gain a reputation as a calm, reasonable person, and your self-respect will blossom.

Chapter 12:
CBT and Mindfulness

Our minds ideally should concentrate on the task at hand except that they occasionally veer off and bring in everyone and everything they meet on the way. Have you ever been working on a project then your mind goes fishing for what would possibly go wrong or what someone thinks of you or the failures that came with the last project? You find yourself having moved from the task at hand to concentrate on those things that the mind brought in, yet you know they will cause you stress, anxiety, and self-doubt. You can benefit from a CBT technique, called Mindfulness-Based Cognitive Therapy (MBCT).

What Is MBCT?

MBCT is a technique that works by combining mindfulness strategies with cognitive-behavioral techniques in helping you understand and manage your emotions and thoughts better and get a reprieve from any distressing feelings. The technique works well for a variety of mental illnesses.

During psychotherapy, you combine cognitive therapy, mindfulness, and meditation. Mindfulness refers to a state of focusing on being acutely aware of what you are feeling and sensing presently without judgment or interruption. Throughout the process, you will learn to recognize and understand your feelings and thought patterns, then you can create new and more effective ones.

In most cases, MBCT works as a group intervention lasting up to eight weeks, and, I must say, the time is worth it. You are required to have a two-hour weekly course and a day-long class sometime after the fifth week. While some of the learning happens in the session, most of the practice happens outside the sessions. You will have to do some homework that may include listening to guided meditations and cultivating mindfulness in your activities by applying the MBCT skills. You also get to learn the three-minute breathing space.

Three-Minute Breathing Space

Usually, this is a quick exercise that is done in three steps:

1. In the first minute, you ask yourself, "How am I doing right now?" while observing your experience and trying to find the right words for those thoughts, sensations, and feelings.

2. During the second minute, you focus on the breath.

3. You spend the last minute expanding your attention from just your breath to the physical sensations and their effect on your body.

How Does It Work?

Through MBCT, you can tackle those intrusive thoughts by learning to use mindfulness mediation in disrupting the processes that often trigger those thoughts and emotions.

Allowing such thoughts to happen leads to low mood, weariness, sluggishness, and negative thoughts taking over and that makes you anxious and depressed. Worse is that even after such an episode, there are chances that you may feel blue, and small other things, like fatigue, can easily trigger another episode.

In this technique, you learn to recognize that you are a separate entity from your mood and thought, giving you a sense of being. Understanding that your thoughts and emotions do not define you can help you allow you to be liberated from negative thought patterns that may be playing on repeat mode in your head. You begin to appreciate your thoughts and emotions but also know that they are separate from you and although they can both exist simultaneously, they do not have to lead you where they please. You can go in the opposite direction—into the land of positivity—which disarms the negative ones. You are the one who matters, the one who decides what to give power to.

You also learn various skills in MBCT that help you in combating those low, blue, and depressive thoughts and symptoms as they arise. Learning MBCT skills helps you to have your own army and strategies that you can refer to when you feel like the mental battlefield is getting hot or overwhelming. Besides, knowing that you are prepared for such times of intrusive thoughts, anxiety and depression give you confidence in your ability to deal with them, making you approach things from a winner's perspective.

Benefits of MBCT

There are many benefits of MBCT. Some of them include:

- Helps you discover your own mood and thought patterns.

- Helps you learn how to focus on the present and enjoy the small pleasures of life.

- Teaches you how to stop the downward spiral that comes with painful memories and bad moods.

- Learning how to shift to a balanced and non-judgmental mental state.

- Improved physical health, since most of the techniques include some form of exercise.

- Reduced stress that comes with focusing on the present and soothing exercises, like yoga.

- Improved concentration on tasks, increasing your chances of succeeding.

- Improved overall mood.

- Better ability to face the challenges of life.

MBCT Techniques

Other MBCT techniques include:

Body Scan

Earlier on, we touched on the body scan. Here, you lie on your back with palms up and feet slightly apart or you sit comfortably on a chair with your feet on the floor. You have to stay very still during this exercise and only move deliberately, fully aware if you need to adjust your position.

Next, with the help of the facilitator, you bring awareness to your breath, taking note of the rhythm of inhaling and exhaling. Now, move attention to your body, take in everything about it, including how it feels, the clothing texture, temperature, contours of the surface you are lying on, and the entire environment. Once you have mastered that, focus your attention on any part of the body that is feeling light, heavy, sore, or even tingly. Move any parts where you feel no sensation.

Scan the entire body, starting from the toes, paying attention to how each body part feels. Move up to the rest of the foot, up the legs, and all the way to the top of the head. Once you finish scanning every bit of your body, gently bring back awareness to the room where you are, opening your eyes slowly and moving to a comfortable sitting position.

Mindful Stretching

You have to bring mindfulness to your situations, and one way of doing so is incorporating it into your stretching. Before you rush to exercise, take time to have some mindful stretching, which prepares both your body and mind for the upcoming physical exertion. Besides, mindful stretching can help increase your sense of balance and awareness. Below are some mindful-stretching options you can try.

1. **Pandiculation:** This means a fairly simple stretch. All you have to do is place your palms on your shoulders, raise your elbows to the height of the shoulders, then open your mouth to let out a satisfying yawn.

2. **Yoga poses:** The four main ones are:

   a. **Side-to-side neck stretch:** Sit and gently use your hand to pull the neck from side to side.

   b. **Gomukhasana:** Open your chest as you extend the triceps and shoulders while sitting cross-legged or kneeling.

   c. **Pigeon pose:** Your hips should be on the floor with one leg in front of you and perpendicular to the mat. The other leg stays straight out behind you.

   d. **The scorpion:** Start by lying flat with your arms stretched out to the side. Lift your right foot high, keeping your sole straight up to the ceiling before lifting the right hip too. Now, move the lifted foot to the outside of the other leg, while keeping your arms and chest on the floor. You can then switch legs.

Mindful Showering

When you are just beginning, this is a good place to start, incorporating mindfulness in your daily activities. Give attention to the water temperature as it touches your body, feeling the spray, smell of the soap, and the sensation of the lathered soap. If your mind begins to wander, as is common, steer it back to the present by focusing on what you are hearing, feeling, seeing, and smelling.

Mindful Eating

Similarly, this involves giving all your attention to what you are eating. It helps if you can turn off things, like the TV, phone, or radio, that are disruptive, so you can focus just on eating. Feel the texture of the food, concentrate on the aroma and the taste.

Mindfully Brushing Teeth

Don't laugh. Keeping in the present is important, and what better way to do so than focusing on the everyday activities that you undertake, especially brushing your teeth? Focus your attention on the strokes of the brush, their movement, and the feel on your teeth and gums. Give attention to the taste of the toothpaste and how it feels in your mouth.

In essence, you can incorporate mindfulness into all areas of life and your daily activities. By doing so, you learn to focus on the present, filter your thoughts to what you want them to be, and, hence, exercise control over your thoughts and emotions. The main idea with mindfulness is not to change what you are doing but rather to pay attention and notice what you are doing. Gone will be the days you drove home and can't remember taking the last three turns or eating and not remembering the food's taste.

Learning to incorporate mindfulness in my life has helped keep me in the present, helping me appreciate the coffee, the sunshine, the flowers, and all the simple beautiful things that life has to offer. I practice mindfulness so much in my daily life that it has become a part of me. When I feel those intrusive thoughts and anxiety about issues creeping in, I switch them off through mindfulness. I no longer go for coffee with a friend and spend the time worrying about work or things I haven't done. No, I sit there in the present, engage in the conversation, savor the coffee and the activities around the coffee shop. After that, I am glad I went out. I get to laugh, enjoy some good company, and generally feel good. You should try it.

Conclusion

Once a person has suffered from a mental health issue, it is more than likely that this issue is going to be an ongoing, lifetime consideration. But fear not. Since you have made your way through this book, you have already taken several steps that are vital when facing down the beast that is your mental health issues. The steps, practices, and exercises described in this book are not actions meant to be taken once to resolve what you have been going through. You have been thinking, behaving, and labeling your experiences for a good amount of your life, so it is going to take time for you to permanently shift those habits into the opposing direction. Try to think of it like a person who has asthma, or a broken leg; it is going to take time to heal yourself, but along the way, you will have learned new methods that align with the particular issue you are combating against.

Mental health recovery is not a phrase that connotes the vanquishing of symptoms. Participating in your mental health recovery means that you no longer want to be a slave to your mental disorder, and are making a proactive choice to change. This is exactly what you have done while going through this workbook. You have committed yourself to make your life better, all while cultivating new and healthier habits. But that does not mean that you should stop practicing the skills mentioned in this book. Once you have climbed over the hurdle of mental health recovery, comes the point of mental health maintenance. Maintenance is a lifelong task, but it does not have to be as daunting as it sounds. External and internal events in your life may try to flush out the presence of your disorder or cause an unexpected flare-up. Descending back into the old habits of your mental disorder is nothing to be ashamed of. But this is why practicing maintenance throughout your life is important; it wards off the abrupt rising of your old ways of thinking, as well as prepares you for the unpredictability of life.

It may take more than one read of this workbook to begin integrating the skills into your mind. Participating in constant exposures, cognitive restructuring, and breathing techniques are some of the ways that you are going to gain more of an understanding of what you are going through. Going through this book with a therapist, physician, family, friend or spouse is a good way to begin sharing your experiences with them and opening lines of communication. This is going to be helpful should you require the aid of someone if you are feeling extreme panic, depression, or anger.

Other practices that have been proven to help people recover from mental health practices are the application of exercise, the observation of eating habits, and the tracking of sleep patterns. These are all factors that could affect a person's mood, anxiety, or rise in anger at a particular moment.

But most importantly, learn to be kind, patient, and compassionate with yourself. Think of your mental health issues as an experience of walking along a path you did not have a map for. You had no idea what was going on within you, and now, with the support of family and friends, you are slowly learning to draw your own map and the direction in which your life will lead. Mental health is not a curse, nor is it an experience that is uncommon. One in three people that you meet in your life have at some point suffered from a mental health disorder. Mental health is just as important as physical health; the two works in tandem. Mental health issues have long been mystified as something akin to the supernatural. But scientists, health physicians, and thousands upon thousands of studies throughout the world have proven otherwise. Mental health issues are the combination of brain-behavior, external behavior, and learned thinking styles that sometimes work together to create an overall negative experience for the individual. But now, you have the weapons to fight back against it.

9 781915 078278